R. P. Hinks

GREEK AND ROMAN PORTRAIT SCULPTURE

Published for
THE TRUSTEES OF THE BRITISH MUSEUM
by British Museum Publications Limited

© 1976, The Trustees of the British Museum

ISBN 0 7141 1252 6 *cased*

ISBN 0 7141 1253 4 *paper*

First published 1935

Published by British Museum Publications Ltd.,
6 Bedford Square, London WC1B 3RA

Designed by Wendy Bann
Set in 11/13 Baskerville and printed in Great Britain by
J. W. Arrowsmith Limited, Bristol and London.

PREFACE TO THE SECOND EDITION

Roger Hinks, who died in 1963 at the age of sixty, was an Assistant Keeper in the Department of Greek and Roman Antiquities from 1926 to 1939. Educated at Westminster, where he was a King's Scholar, and at Trinity College, Cambridge, he went out to Rome after taking his degree and worked there for two years as private secretary to Mrs Arthur Strong, at that time Assistant Director of the British School. These two Roman years were decisive for his scholarly development. An ardent propagandist of *Romanità* in all its forms, Mrs Strong aroused in him a lasting interest in Roman art; and under her aegis he made contacts with many distinguished continental archaeologists, especially German and Austrian, from whom he learnt to approach ancient art as an historian rather than an antiquarian, and to regard it as an integral part of humanistic studies. On his return to England he took his place naturally in the ranks of those younger scholars who in their various fields were working for the recognition of art-history as a legitimate academic discipline in this country.

Of the publications which Hinks produced during his time in the Museum the best-known is probably his *Carolingian Art*, which appeared in 1935. As the writer notes in his Introduction to the American edition of 1962, the aim of this work was 'to make clear to the generation brought up on Boeckler, Köhler, Goldschmidt, and Zimmerman the findings of the generation brought up on Riegl and Strzygowski'; in other words, to show that the 'antique' on which the Carolingian *renovatio* was based, was a far more heterogeneous and multifarious phenomenon than students of the latter had hitherto assumed. Hinks's debt to German scholarship is everywhere apparent in *Carolingian Art*; and it is perhaps his most important achievement that he found a way—invented a language, one might almost say—in which German art-historical thought could be intelligibly transmitted to the minds of Anglo-Saxon art-historians and archaeologists.

But that is not to imply that he accepted German scholarship indiscriminately: his essay ' "Classical" and "Classicistic" in the Criticism of Ancient Art' (*Kritische Berichte*, VI, 1937) contains shrewd comments on the *Grundbegriffe* of the great Wölfflin, then recently introduced to a somewhat mystified British public in Hottinger's translation (1932).

Hinks's historical and humanistic approach to ancient art is no less evident in his two official Museum publications. The first to appear was his *Catalogue of Paintings and Mosaics*, 1933, which contains a penetrating essay on two-dimensional representation in ancient art, a remarkable achievement for a young man of thirty. This was followed two years later by the work reprinted here, his *Greek and Roman Portrait-Sculpture*, 1935. Based on examples in the Museum's collection, it is an excellent guide, meticulous without being pedantic; but what gives it its special value is the writer's psychological insight, his awareness of the changing spiritual situation, of which good portraits are the vivid expression. As a concise introduction to the history of ancient portraiture Hinks's essay could hardly be bettered; and it is a measure of the thoroughness and good judgment of his scholarship that despite all the work that has been done on the subject in the last forty years, there is nothing of consequence that one would wish to change in it.

D. E. L. HAYNES
Keeper of Greek and Roman Antiquities

LIST OF ILLUSTRATIONS

The numbers in brackets refer to A. H. Smith's *Catalogue of Sculpture in the Department of Greek and Roman Antiquities*. London: British Museum, 3 vols., 1892–1904.

68 Caracalla (1917).
69 Unknown Roman woman (2009).
70 Julia Mamaea (1922).
71 Unknown Roman (1953).
72 Unknown Roman (1921).
73 Unknown Roman (1968).
74 Unknown Roman (1959).

I

THE early history of the portrait is bound up with the history of religious belief. A faith in the survival of an intact personality is an indispensable condition for the development of true portraiture; and in ancient times times we find real portraits only in societies where such a faith was strongly held. In Egypt, for example, the general tendency of art was to establish rigid types and to repeat them almost unchanged for centuries; yet parallel with this conservative habit ran an individualistic tradition of portraiture which was responsible for many remarkable achievements and some incomparable masterpieces.

Such portraits, however, are not to be taken as proving that the Egyptians felt a modern detached curiosity about the facial peculiarities of this or that individual. Even at that moment when the cult of the Egyptian gods was abandoned by Akhenaten, who worshipped the sun alone, we are not to attribute the unrivalled portraits of the heretical king and his family found in his city at El-Amarna to the mere desire for a speaking likeness. Behind these, as behind all Egyptian portraits, lies a magical requirement, to the satisfaction of which the craftsman devoted the best of his energy and skill. The Egyptian believed that when he died his soul looked about for a substitute which it might inhabit and reanimate; and that if it found none, it would wander away and be lost for ever. It was most important, therefore, to make a statue which resembled the living man as closely as possible, in order that the soul might recognize its own corporeal shape, and the personality of the individual survive the dissolution of his mortal body. This desire for personal continuity explains also the practice of mummification and the use of the painted or modelled mask to take the place of the human features; and it accounts for the discrepancy between the stylized forms of the gods and divinized kings and the carefully particularized traits of the private individual. There are, indeed, cases where two entirely different statues bearing the same name

9

have been found in the same tomb; and in some circumstances it would seem as though the name alone were a sufficient identification mark. Nevertheless, it is generally true to say that the magical necessity for an accurate likeness impressed itself with great stringency upon the Egyptian imagination in view of its preoccupation with religious provision.

Nowhere else do we find the same preoccupation with religious portraiture. In Sumeria the effigies signed with the names of kings and queens are commemorative in intention and conventional in form. Burial customs required an elaborate equipment of objects designed for the well-being of the dead man in the tomb; but no realistic image was needed to enable the ghost to recognize its proper body. So also in Crete and on the Aegean mainland the dead man received worship and offerings, but there are hardly any signs of a tradition of portraiture. The gold masks placed on the faces of the bodies found by Schliemann in the fourth shaft-grave at Mycenae represent the man as dead, with closed eyes; and thus, so far from creating an illusion of immortality, they underline his mortal state. It is clear that the Mycenaean had no very lively hopes of a personal survival.

We are reminded of the Homeric world, where Anticleia tells her son Odysseus how the strength of a man ebbs away from his bones and flesh and his soul hovers like a dream by night; and where the ghosts of Penelope's suitors twitter like bats as Hermes leads them to the shades. The Greeks inherited this unsubstantial world, where the spirits retained nothing but the memory of what they once had been, and where the individual was neither his full self nor merged in some universal consciousness. With such expectations it is not surprising that the funerary art of the Greeks looked backward to the real world, and took on a commemorative and mythological complexion. This tendency to dwell upon the past rather than to provide for the future, to regard as piety the remembrance of something gone rather than the service of something present, explains why the classical art of Greece idealized the man in general terms instead of fastening upon his accidental characteristics; and why the portrait, as we know it and as the Egyptians and the Romans knew it, appears so late in Greece.

Pausanias says that shortly after the fifty-fourth Olympiad
(564 B.C.) the people of Phigaleia erected a stone statue of
Arrhachion the athlete in the archaic style, with the feet hardly
separated and the arms hanging down the side of the hips. It had
once borne an inscription, but by the time of Pausanias this was
erased. Evidently this memorial statue of Arrhachion resembled
the so-called *kouroi*, formerly thought to be figures of Apollo and
now regarded as mainly votive, though partly also commemorative and sepulchral. A similar votive type is the seated effigy of
Chares (B 278 in the Archaic Room: *c.* 540 B.C.); its head is lost, *1*
but its body resembles those of its companions which lined the
sacred way at Branchidae, near Miletus in Asia Minor. Only the
inscription distinguishes it essentially from its neighbours: 'I am
Chares, son of Kleisis, ruler of Teichioussa. The statue is
Apollo's.' The fact that the statue belongs to the god is more
important than the fact that it commemorates a human personage. It is a symbol of Chares, but not a portrait, because it lays no
stress upon the attributes which belonged to him alone.

The grave-reliefs, which extend continuously from the mid- *2*
dle of the sixth century B.C. to the end of the fourth, adopt the
same generalized and symbolical mode of expression. They bear
witness to the facial types in vogue during those seven genera-
tions, but of actual portraiture they contain hardly a trace. So
slight is the personal reference, so persistently does every man
resemble his contemporaries, that we begin to think that they
must have been purchased ready-made and distinguished only
by the inscriptions, and possibly by the choice of an attribute.
This colourless similarity, so noticeable after the lively differenti-
ation of Egyptian portrait-sculpture, prompts the question: Did
the Greeks all look alike to each other? And if not, why did they
plane down the differences between one man and another and
reduce all their several features to a single pattern?

To answer this question it is necessary to make a short
excursion into the history of psychology. Technical conditions
do not explain this unwillingness to particularize. On the con-
trary, it is precisely the inexpert craftsman who is most likely to
hit upon those accidental irregularities of outline which produce
a superficial appearance of portraiture, and even of caricature.

1 Chares.

2 Stele of Glykylla.

From the beginning of Greek vase-painting we find occasional profiles expressively individualized; but such independent experiments are not encouraged. By the beginning of the sixth century stock formulas to suit various physiognomic types start to be developed, and are repeated uniformly at any given stage until the formal sense itself changes. Within each generation, indeed, the formula varies according to the artist's requirements, but not necessarily according to the suggestions of nature itself. The instinct to discipline the casual appearances of life in obedience to a preconceived ideal was too strong to allow the artist as yet to investigate and exploit individual phenomena.

In the fifth century we begin to detect the first traces of curiosity about the individual, the earliest tentative essays in true

3 portraiture. The terminal bust of Pericles (549), of which the original was perhaps by Cresilas, is the standard example of the idealized likeness, as understood by the masters of the classical period. Accustomed as we are to the sharp accents of modern portraiture, we are inclined to regard it as an exercise in physiognomy rather than a real character-study. The artist has started with the known personality of Pericles, and has set out to excogitate the type of perfect statesman and embody it in a plastic shape; he has not accepted the features of the actual man as his primary data and given them an artistic unity, as a modern portraitist would be bound to do. The bust is consequently an abstraction. So vague are the indications given by the marble features that were it not for the inscription we should hardly have guessed that they were meant to recall an historical personage; we should have perceived only a collection of traits designed to suggest a number of edifying virtues, but not the unique amalgam which we call a personality. We may call the head a noble invention: a 'character', in the Theophrastan sense. But it is not a portrait.

It might be supposed that this emptiness of human content was the fault of the copyist, and the original would have been more vivid and authentic; but this is not to be taken for granted.

4 The earliest effigies on Greek coins, such as the heads of satraps on the issues of Cyzicus, Colophon, and other cities in Asia Minor, are not so much studies of individuals as barbarian

3 Pericles.

4 Tissaphernes, Satrap of Caria.
Silver tetradrachm.

5 Mausolus.

formulas. The deviation from the ideal norm is racial, not personal. Just as the figures of old people and foreigners on Greek vases appear at first sight to show a sharpness of definition which the indigenous and youthful figures lack, so these Persians have a new quality which we are inclined to call portraiture. But an examination of several specimens will convince us that their facial peculiarities belong to their race, not to themselves.

Yet it is perhaps not a pure accident that our nearest approach as yet to genuine portraiture should bring us into contact with non-Greeks once more; and this suspicion is at once confirmed in the first monumental effigy which gives us a secure starting-point for our investigations. The figures of Mausolus and Artemisia from the Mausoleum at Halicarnassus date from about 350 B.C. Originally they stood, not on the top of the building (as was formerly supposed), but inside, like deities in the cella of a temple. The treatment is worthy of this impressive setting. The king and queen stand side by side, solemn figures in drapery of an ideal amplitude. The face of Artemisia is destroyed, except for the forehead with its triple row of artificial curls. The features of Mausolus, on the other hand, are well 5 preserved. His head is inclined to one side; and he wears an oriental moustache and a beard covering the cheeks and the chin, and long straight hair falling on his shoulders behind. His eyes are deep-set, and have a distant, melancholy look in them. When we compare this version of an oriental prince with those on the coins of the preceding generation we notice the distinct 4 progress made towards the realization of a personality in plastic shape. The features of Mausolus are, indeed, somewhat generalized, in accordance with the demands of the monumental scale; but the cast of countenance, the poise of the head, and the whole rhythm of the body combine to create the impression of a real individual. Portraiture, as we understand it, has begun.

The first portrait which we can claim as a masterpiece is thus the effigy of a Carian prince and not of a Greek citizen. It seems as though portraits were lacking hitherto as much because there was no demand for them as because the Greek artist was disinclined to experiment with such a form. But from now onwards this reluctance is overcome, and the sculptors of the fourth century showed a considerable interest in the representation of an historic personality as an artistic genre. This enrichment of the subject-matter of Greek art is probably an outcome of the invention of the soul as a psychological fact, which is attributed by the historians of philosophy to Socrates. Hitherto when a Greek spoke of his 'self' he meant his body, the centre of life and consciousness. It was Socrates who discovered that the real self is not the body but the soul. This fundamental change of mind found its reflex in due course. The dramatists began to explore human problems from the inside outwards, and the artists to experiment with the rendering of the emotions. It is worth noting, however, that Pliny, describing Silanion's statue of the choleric bronze-worker Apollodorus, expressly calls it 'not a man, but Anger itself'. This should warn us against confusing the desire to render various emotions and physical states with the desire to create an individualized portrait. Preparations were assuredly being made, both in psychology and technique, for the foundation of a genuine tradition of portraiture, but the moment was not yet due.

Few of the busts of philosophers and poets who lived before the time of Alexander the Great are contemporary likenesses, and fewer still, perhaps, can claim to be physically trustworthy.
6 The Sophocles, of which we possess a version in marble (1831) as well as the famous bronze brought back from Constantinople in the seventeenth century by the Earl of Arundel (Bronze 847), is an imaginative creation of the Hellenistic period. The Euripides
7 (1833) has been traced back to the statue set up in 340 B.C., with others of Aeschylus and Sophocles, in the theatre at Athens. Of other busts representing personages of the late fifth and early
8 fourth centuries, the inscribed herm of Aeschines (1839) and the
9 satyr-like head of Socrates (1837) give the impression of deriving from types invented about the middle of the fourth century; they show the compactness of design, with the hair lying close to the skull, the shallow set of the eyes with broad and rather flat upper lids, the sharp metallic definition of the lips, and the generalized modelling typical of pre-Hellenistic sculpture. On
10 the other hand, the Demosthenes (1840) is more crisply individualized and might well be a copy of the head of the statue by

6 Sophocles.

7 Euripides.

8 Aeschines.

9 Socrates.

10 Demosthenes.

11 Antisthenes.

Polyeuctus commissioned in 280 B.C. The romantically expressive head of Antisthenes (1838) is based upon a type probably *11* created at least a hundred years after the death of the founder of the Cynic school of philosophy, which happened about 380 B.C. A sculptor of the first half of the fourth century could hardly have designed this picturesque mass of hair, with the great lock tumbling over the forehead, these deep-set eyes shadowed by irregularly jutting brows, and this boldly unideal nose. The originator of this fine conception must have been one of the foremost artists of the early Hellenistic period. Other imaginary types of earlier historical characters created in the third century may probably be traced in the two rather similar heads of poets (1830 and 1851), the former traditionally called 'Alcaeus'. *13 14*

The rapid development of portraiture in the second half of the fourth century coincides with the interpenetration of Hellenic and oriental ideas which accompanied the conquests of Alexander the Great; but the outward appearance of the conqueror himself has survived only in a veiled and doubtful shape. We know that he took pains to have his features recorded only by artists of the first rank, and that he is said to have given exclusive rights to the painter Apelles, the sculptor Lysippus, and the gem-engraver Pyrgoteles; but no traces of their style can be detected with any certainty in the existing portraits. It is doubtful whether any of these are contemporary, and all appear to be more or less idealized and divinized. The head from Alexandria (1857) has some of the features mentioned in the literary *16* descriptions, such as the leonine mass of hair, the upward glance, the melting look in the eyes, and the bend of the neck; but the impression is not individual, and it is probable that the king was represented here as some divinity, perhaps a sea-god. Even less characteristic is the much-worn head (1839) which seems to reproduce a slightly different prototype.

The coin-portraits of Alexander are less reliable as an iconographic guide than might have been expected. They are untouched originals, it is true, but none are contemporary. The earliest and best is the noble head on the tetradrachms of *15* Lysimachus issued about twenty years after Alexander's death; yet this represents not the man but the divinized son of Ammon,

12 Chrysippus.

13 Greek poet.

14 Greek poet.

15 Alexander the Great.
Silver tetradrachm.

16 Alexander the Great.

as is shown by the ram's horns in the hair. It has been suggested that this beautiful head was borrowed from a gem by Pyrgoteles: certainly a great artist was responsible for it. Only the pose of the head, however, the expressive glance from the deep-set eye, and the mane of hair are the authentic marks of the Alexander type, and these general traits rather look back to the earlier conception of the Greek portrait as an ideal reconstruction, than suggest that Alexander's own effigies made an immediate contribution to Hellenistic portraiture.

This genre made rapid progress, however, in the first half of the third century. We have noted the Antisthenes and the Demosthenes as indicating a new trend even in the imaginative reconstruction of earlier worthies; the portraits of contemporaries show even more distinctly that interest in peculiarities of feature and gesture which is the essential condition for a real
17 likeness. The head of Epicurus (1843) is probably copied from an original made about the time of his death, which took place in 270 B.C. We know from Cicero and Pliny that the Epicureans used to set up portraits of their founder in their meeting-places and carry them about wherever they went, sacrificing to them on the twentieth day of the month in honour of Epicurus' birthday. This practice, which may also have obtained in other sects, would explain why so many replicas of philosopher-types have sur-
18, 12 vived; the Metrodorus (1845) and the Chrysippus (1846) are characteristic examples of this very frequent class. It would also account for the existence of small portable bronze replicas such
19 as the seated statuette (Bronze 848) supposed by some authorities to represent the Cyrenaic philosopher Aristippus and by others Zeno, the founder of the Stoic school.

A statuette of this kind, with its easy and natural position of the head, arms, and crossed legs, shows a perfect mastery not only of anatomical representation but also of the more initmate study of psychology. It also illustrates the Greek conception of the whole body as a single expressive unit. Taken by itself the face might seem a little empty and non-committal, but regarded, as the Greeks regarded it, as but one of the many members, it takes its place to perfection in the general rhythm of the body. This attitude to the face, so different from that of the Romans and of

17 Epicurus.

18 Metrodorus.

19 Greek philosopher.

20 Antiochus I. Soter.   Silver tetradrachm.

21   Philetaerus of Pergamon.   Silver tetradrachm.

ourselves—due to the sharp distinction we make between the naked and the clothed parts of the body, and so different also from the half-magical sense of the countenance that gives the Egyptian portrait its compelling power, explains why the heads of so many Greek statues, when taken out of their context, are apt to strike us as lifeless and lacking in character.

In spite of this general truth, however, there developed in the Hellenistic period a feeling for essential character which showed itself perfectly capable of self-realization. This sense of character operates from within. It achieves its effects not by a literal reproduction of the external features, with all their blemishes and irregularities, but by a sort of irradiation of the total personality throughout its physical envelope. The individual accidents are exploited not for their own sake, as a Roman would have exploited them, but for their symbolic value as indices of temperament.

In this respect the later series of Hellenistic coins offer us admirable examples of psychological portraiture, in which facial oddities are adroitly used to accentuate the personal characteristics of the subject. The double chins and beaky nose of Antiochus I, the fleshy jowl and shrewd little pig-like eyes of the [20] eunuch Philetaerus, the handsome, truculent profile of [21] Orophernes of Cappadocia, and the curious half grim and half [22] humorous mouth of Antimachus of Bactria are seized upon with [23] almost a caricaturist's eye for essentials and stated with a telling economy of means. Such a power of abstraction, indispensable in the confined space of a coin or a gem, is, in fact, no less necessary to the maker of life-sized effigies, exposed as he is to the temptation of purely empirical copying. A considerable intellectual effort is needed to reduce the myriad wrinkles and inequalities of the human face, with all its contrasts of colour and texture, to a reasonable and coherent plastic construction, and at the same time to retain the impress of a human personality; and this effort is greatly assisted by a natural propensity to see the object in its most general terms, and not in too sharp a focus. The superiority of a Hellenistic portrait over its Roman counterpart, regarded simply as a sculptural composition, lies in that even diffusion of interest over the whole surface and in that determi-

33

22 Orophernes of Cappadocia.   Silver tetradrachm.

23 Antimachus of Bactria.   Silver tetradrachm.

nation not to be seduced by detail, however curious and rich in character.

This technical restraint is most conspicuous in bronze, the pliable and accommodating nature of which leads an artist of less scrupulous taste into all sorts of pitfalls. A fine Hellenistic bronze head like the African from Cyrene (Bronze 268) shows how far it 24 is possible to combine an imitative treatment of texture with the broader and more abstract requirements of metalwork as a fine art. This head is remarkable for its success in balancing elaborate detail-treatment against a simple and harmonious general effect. The curly hair is intricately disposed in wavy sequences of locks radiating from the crown of the head, each lock being built up with careful attention to its structure and growth, so that the whole mass of hair coheres like a living organism. In the same way the underlying framework of the face is steadily borne in mind and so easily supports the rich and varied handling of the parts: the chased beard and eyebrows, and the separately inset lips, eyes, and eyelashes. This minute concern for detail, involving frequent changes of scale and various kinds of technique, is justified because the artist never relaxes his grasp of the large tectonic relationships, such as the covering of flesh and muscle over the jaw and the cap of hair which springs from the skull.

This broad contrast between polished flesh and rough hair, upon whose balanced interaction the aesthetic effect of the head depends, is seen in another Hellenistic masterpiece, a head of an African in green slate from Alexandria. The expert handling of 25 this very hard material suggests that the sculptor was either a Hellenized Egyptian or a Greek who had learnt his craft in an Egyptian workshop; the technique is Egyptian, but the actual conception of form is Hellenic. The nature of the stone and the processes used for cutting and grinding it give all the planes a sharpness and simplicity which would be less appropriate to the pale translucent colour and the softer crystalline texture of marble. The lustrous dark green surface, reflecting every nuance of light and shadow with perfect clarity, imposes a strict discipline on the artist; too much detail would break the beauty of the even finish, and attempts at contrasts of colour would result only in confusion and vulgarity. The distinction between

24 Head of an African.

25 Unknown Egyptian.

the relatively dark polished flesh and the relatively light unpolished hair is the utmost permissible. The concentration on severe simplicity and the refusal to attempt transitory effects of expression are a tribute to the respect which the sculptor felt for the monumental quality of his material, though they also reflect the survival of the classical taste throughout the Hellenistic period side by side with the romantic impressionism derived from Scopas and Praxiteles.

26   That such classicism was not dictated by the material alone is clear from a contemporary head of a Hellenistic ruler found at Cyrene (1383). This portrait shows the same advanced stylization of the features, from which all picturesque accidents have been planed away, the same treatment of the hair as a compact area of uniform texture sharply contrasted with the smooth flesh, and the same classical calm of demeanour. Yet in spite of the subdued tone and the rigour with which non-essentials are suppressed the head remains unmistakably a portrait. The structure of the skull—notably the great width of the brow compared with the close set of the eyes and the shortness of the mouth— and the evidently deliberate asymmetry of the features when seen obliquely from above are evidently due to the peculiarities of an individual model.

We may conjecture that this classicizing tradition in Hellenistic portraiture is derived from Lysippus and his brother Lysistratus, who is said by Pliny to have been the first to make portraits with the assistance of life-casts, which he afterwards moulded in wax and then retouched before casting them in bronze. It is easy to believe that the bronze head from Cyrene was made in this way; the actual proportions seem to be almost mechanically set out, and the exercise of the artist's judgement seems to be confined to the harmonious management of the surface-detail.

The impressionist tradition, on the other hand, develops out of the inventions of Scopas and Praxiteles. The study of facial play and gesture was greatly extended by the early Hellenistic portraitists, who began to desert the older Greek principle of distributing the expression over the whole body and took to concentrating it on the head, like a Roman or a modern sculptor. This psychological tendency makes the impressionists a livelier

26 Hellenistic ruler.

27 group than their classicizing contemporaries. In spite of its damaged surface the ivy-crowned head (1852) has a distinctly personal look; this is conveyed by the twist of the neck, the casual notation of the features, and the almost wilfully informal treatment of the hair, which is simply blocked out, as though to distract the spectator's attention from the real material structure of the head and to oblige him to consider it as just a modulated mass of a certain colour and texture. This pictorial conception of form, appealing first to the eye, as opposed to the classical principle of appealing to the touch, emerges about the middle of the fourth century and may have been invented by Praxiteles.

29 The actual method of a Hellenistic impressionist may be conveniently studied in a head from Rhodes (1965), whose surface, in spite of superficial damage, is well preserved. The flesh of the face is subtly finished and its pulpy substance is skilfully suggested without any literal imitation of the epidermis, 60 such as was later attempted by Antonine sculptors (cf. 1949). The hair, worked with the drill and hacked out with a broad chisel, appears at first sight to be unfinished, like the drapery round the neck; but when the head is seen from the proper distance the coarse manipulation produces exactly the effect of thick and rather soft hair. The use and abuse of this technical trick in modern times is familiar enough; it is interesting to notice its first appearance in the sculpture of the later Hellenistic period.

From about the middle of the second century B.C. we can detect an effort to combine the formal precision of the classicizing school with the dramatic vivacity of the impressionists. The 30 head of a woman of Levantine type (1873), which dates from about 50 B.C., is finished all over with an even accuracy which classes it among the productions of the classicists, while the sensuous treatment of the flesh shows equally clearly the technical influence of impressionism. The material of this head, a fine-grained limestone, has taken on a soft finish which gives it a certain fluidity of form not intended by the artist. But a similar 31 quality is observable in a contemporary marble head from Cyprus (1879*), a work which shows the art of the late Hellenistic portraitist to the best advantage. The ascetic features, which display the bony structure of the skull under the thin envelope of

40

27 Hellenistic personage as Dionysos.

28 Head of Hellenistic portrait-statue.

29 Unknown Hellenistic personage.

30 Unknown Levantine woman.

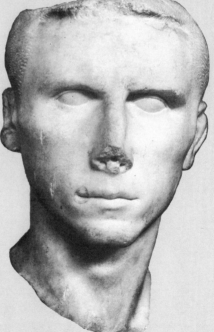

31 Unknown Roman.

flesh, are modelled with perfect assurance and a fine sense of their suggestiveness as an index of character. The head of the
28 portrait-statue from Priene (1152) is comparable with the head from Cyprus, and is probably of the same date. It shows a similar combination of Greek suavity and Roman power. In many of the pure Roman heads, to which we now must turn, this suavity is sacrificed to power; the native Roman sculptor was mainly interested in expression, and where we notice exceptional plastic sensibility or technical brilliance Hellenistic influence may be suspected.

2

THE Italic portrait, like the Egyptian, is the result of a ritual practice. For magic reasons it was necessary to preserve the features of departed ancestors; and the effigies which played a part in the funeral ceremonies, and were preserved in the atrium of the family house, must certainly have stimulated the Italic and Roman tradition of portraiture. It would be an exaggeration, however, to assert that all the characteristic effects of Roman portraiture are due to ancestral *imagines*, and still more to ascribe them to the technique of death-masks and the practice of modelling funeral effigies in wax. The real story of their origin is more complex and still remains obscure in many important respects.

In the first place it is necessary to distinguish two strains in early Italic portrait-sculpture because the tension between them produces certain ambiguities in Roman Republican art which are not always correctly interpreted. Of these two strains one is indigenous and the other is imported. The indigenous, or Italic strain proper, is conspicuous for sharpness of characterization and selective emphasis on the salient points of a face. The artist concentrates on expression and leaves construction to take care of itself. The Hellenic practice of building up a head by logical processes akin to those of nature itself is discarded in favour of expressionism, or the creation of vital effects by abstract means. Whereas the Greek was chiefly interested in the physical substance and elaborated each feature in terms of the chosen material, combining the whole by a conscious effort of will, the Italian regarded his material as simply the inert medium for the realization of an idea. The consequence of this difference of approach is that an Italic portrait is more allusive and symbolic than a Greek portrait: a hint at a personality rather than a reconstruction of a body. But the existence of the imported strain in Italic portraiture from an early period means that Hellenistic impressionism had started to work upon Italic naturalism, mitigating its dryness and lending it a consistency of style, some time before the beginning of what can properly be called Roman sculpture. The Romans, in other words, inherited from their predecessors in the peninsula a mixed tradition, in which the Etruscan element was strongly tinged with Hellenism and what we may call the Latin element was comparatively pure and independent.

The effect of this hybrid origin of Italic art may best be seen by comparing two representatives of the opposing tendencies. Let 32 the head of Seianti Hanunia stand for the Hellenizing strain and 33 the votive head of a peasant for the pure Italic stock. In spite of her Etruscan name, there is little that one can call Italic about the tomb effigy of Seianti Hanunia, the wife of Tlesna. Her fleshy features are generalized to suit a preconceived notion of Hellenistic beauty, and the portrait-elements are reduced to a minimum. Italic expressiveness, coarse but genuine, has given way to a rather feeble pastiche of Hellenistic emotionalism. But this loss is balanced by a new interest in structure and the fundamental sculptural relations of which Italic art was originally ignorant. These lessons have been thoroughly learnt by the maker of the votive head, which is a vigorous and successful study of a peasant type. The strong Italic character appears in the large, stern mouth, with a wart on the upper lip, the high and prominent cheek-bones, and the deep-set, observant eyes. The Hellenic training is seen in the complex but coherent design of the hair, which reminds us of that on the bronze head from Cyrene, and generally in the firm logic of the whole composition. By the simplest means, and without much subtlety, yet with a good grip of the sculptor's problem, the maker of this head proves how completely it was possible to make the best of both traditions. Few Hellenistic portraits have the actuality of this masterpiece of popular art, though few Italic works of this period show a like command of technical resources.

33 It may be said that the votive head has a certain reality which is absent from the portrait of Seianti Hanunia. But it would be a mistake to say that realism is a persistent feature of Italic portraiture; and still more would it be wrong to suggest, with some modern writers, that such realism has anything to do with

32 Seianti Hanunia.

33 Italic terracotta votive head.

its magic origins. Realism certainly occurs in Italic art at one phase, but it is a late phase, when the magic aspect of the portrait had been quite forgotten and a rationalistic curiosity about the physical structure of the body had taken its place. Realism, or a detached interest in the actual appearance of things, is a logical consequence of Greek naturalism, and especially of that prosecuted under the influence of Aristotle. Such scientific study of natural phenomena does not appear in Roman art before the end of the second century B.C.; and realistic portraiture, in the proper sense of the word, is a symptom of that Hellenization of Roman intellectual and artistic life which began after the Punic wars and reached its climax in the last century of the Republic. On the other hand, the casual imitation of warts, wrinkles, and other individual peculiarities and deformities is part of the general Italic interest in character, and appears at a much earlier date. This used to be attributed to the study of death-masks and the practice of working up casts from such masks into portraits. But this is by no means a safe general inference; it is clear, of course, that death-masks were used, but their influence is seen rather in the structure of the face, and especially in the prominence of the bones and cartilages, than in the faithful reproduction of surface-irregularities. So far from intensifying wrinkles, death tends rather to smooth them out; and the lively and alert look of the best Italic portraits, due to their interesting use of physiognomic oddity, cannot be due to mechanical dependence on casts from a death-mask. In particular, the firm treatment of the eyes and mouth, which are mainly responsible for the expression, must be a result of deliberate artistic judgement and skill.

At the beginning of the first century B.C., about the time of Sulla, this mixed Greek and Italic tradition of early Republican portraiture was subjected to a new Hellenization, which expressed itself mainly in a technical change. Up till this time Roman portraits had been made either of bronze or of terracotta or of wax: in other words, in plastic materials. Under Greek influence they now began to be carved in marble. This fact alone is responsible for the preponderance of Hellenistic style in the last century of the Republic and its triumph in the official art of the

Augustan period. Pliable clay or wax, and the fluid bronze which perpetuated their quality in metallic form, favoured the indecisive Italic method of approaching a head through the study of expression, whereas the resistant substance of marble practically compels the sculptor to make careful decisions about structure.

The grave-reliefs of L. Ampudius Philomusus and Antistius 35 Sarculo (2275) illustrate the composite style of Roman portrait- 36 sculpture during the last decades of the Republic. The latter, which commemorates a master of the Alban college of the Salian priesthood and his wife (who had been his freed-woman), can be dated by Antistia's hairdressing to the period 50–30 B.C. The busts seem to be imitated from sepulchral *imagines*, perhaps in wax; they show a certain Hellenistic orderliness and facility, though there is no attempt to improve and prettify the homeliness of the features. It looks as if these were based to some extent upon a death-mask; the prominent Adam's apple, the long upper lip, and the awkward junction of the very projecting ears and the skull, contrasted with the conventional rendering of the mouth and eyes, are indications of this. The decorative elements are equally mixed in origin: the fluted niches are supposed to typify the shell upon which the soul floats away to the other world; the surrounding wreath is the *corona triumphalis* of immortality; and the staff between the two niches is a Salian emblem. By comparison the relief of L. Ampudius Philomusus and his wife and daughter, though contemporary, is more strictly Italic in conception and design. The effigies are here not heads or busts, but truncated figures looking over a balustrade, as in a box at the theatre.

With all their differences these sepulchral portraits, and the contemporary head of a peasant-type (1962) which we may 34 compare with them, have something in common which it is easier to realize when we compare them for a moment with the purely Hellenistic style of the head from Cyprus already men- 31 tioned (1879*). Judged by the physique, the subjects are in every instance Romans; but while doing justice to the dry expression and the lean features of his sitter, the Hellenistic artist has managed to enliven the whole surface by the subtlety of his surface treatment, which gives his work an altogether richer

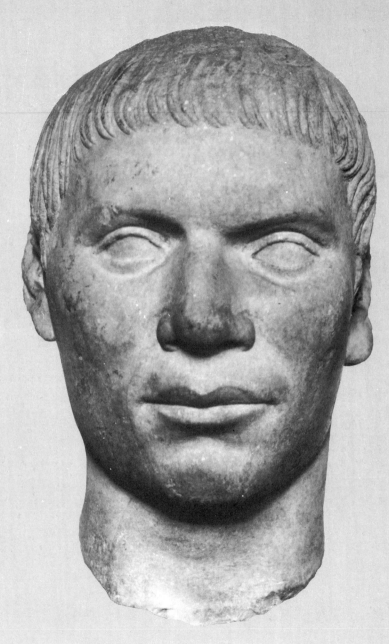

34 Unknown Roman.

35 Grave-relief of L. Ampudius Philomusus.

36 Grave-relief of Antistius Sarculo.

aesthetic interest than the prosaic Roman heads seem to possess.

It is from the Hellenistic, rather than the Italic tradition that the official portraiture of the Augustan school is derived. In spite of the Italian political and cultural programme inaugurated by Augustus, the character of the art designed to give that programme monumental expression is by no means purely Roman. In sentiment and subject it may be so, and it is even possible to detect certain indigenous technical processes in even the most official works, but on the whole Augustus found that the only technique capable of inventing human formulas adequate to his conception of the dignity of his task were those of Hellenistic inspiration. The Roman genius was inventive enough in architecture and the allied decorative arts, but it was not essentially humanistic; consequently it proved much less resourceful than Hellenism in devising mythological and heroic schemes, and less imaginative where portraiture had to convey something more than the mere externals.

Thus it happens that while the portraits of private persons in the Augustan Age do not differ greatly from those of the preceding period, the official art of the State, the court, and the ruling class is sharply distinguished from that which prevailed under the Republic. This is naturally most evident in the adornment of public buildings, but even in the representation of individuals a considerable change can be detected. This may be briefly expressed as a new desire for the heroic. The house of Augustus, however much it might pretend to Republican simplicity, had dynastic ambitions, and these emerge in its conception of portraiture. Its members were to be something more than human, and a certain aloofness at once overshadows their features and bearing. They have lost some of the intimacy of the best Republican types and have gained in return a sustained nobility of style which we must allow to be an impressive achievement.

The head of Augustus (Roman Room), from Meroe on the extreme frontier of Egypt, heroic in size and monumental in design, is thoroughly Roman in its sense of grandeur; but the power to find expression for that sense is Greek. Probably the artist was himself a Greek of Alexandria. The same is very likely

37 The Blacas Cameo of Augustus.

38 Augustus.

39 Antonia—'Clytie'.

true of another portrait, very different in scale but akin in sentiment: the Blacas cameo (Gems 3577). Here Augustus actu- 37 ally wears the diadem of a Hellenistic king, an act which he would never have ventured upon in Rome itself. The marble portraits, on the whole, show him in a more human light. The boyish head (1876) and an unusually delicate version of the grown man (1879) lay stress upon that physical beauty to which 38 Suetonius pays an elaborate tribute (*Divus Augustus*, 79). The same feeling for sensuous charm is seen in the bust of a woman springing from a flower (1874): the so-called Clytie, sometimes 39 identified as Antonia, the daughter of Mark Antony and mother of Germanicus and the emperor Claudius. The unusual style of this remarkably well-preserved bust has more in common with that of gem-engraving than with that of sculpture on a large scale; and as the parallels for the curious shape of the pedestal are terracottas and other objects of a miniature size, it is possible that this portrait is an exceptional essay in larger dimensions by one of the glyptic artists of the period, such as Dioscurides or Herophilus. Of such an essay in the round on a small scale we have an excellent specimen in the plasma head of the elder Agrippina, the grand-daughter of Augustus and the 40 grandmother of Nero (Gems 3946). The beautiful green colour and texture of the stone, which is a silicate of copper, have been skilfully exploited for the sake of their aesthetic effect. The eyes are incised, as in gem-technique, and the ears are pierced for gold earrings. The head may have belonged to a large statuette, the body being made of some material of contrasting colour. Such polychrome sculpture was introduced from Egypt at about this period; the basalt and porphyry used for life-sized statues were imitated on a small scale in even richer and more precious materials.

The classical style introduced in the time of Augustus became even cooler and more precise under his immediate successors; indifferent examples of Julio-Claudian sculpture can be very empty and mechanical, as we see from the head of Claudius 42 (1155) found at Priene. But the better specimens, such as the unusual bearded man (1926), have an elegant, if frigid, assur- 43 ance which shows at least that the sculptors of this period were

40 Agrippina the Elder.

41 The Apotheosis of Marciana.

42 Claudius.

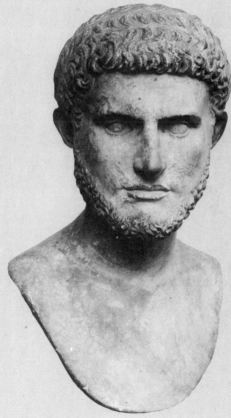

43 Unknown Roman.

masters of all the technical problems of their medium. This portrait may be dated by the shape of the bust and the style of hairdressing to the reign of Nero.

The accession of Vespasian, the downright soldier who made a point of despising the courtly arts and accomplishments, is marked by an Italic revival. Flavian portraits are livelier and more colloquial than the correct and conventional productions of the Julio-Claudian Age. The notation of vivid detail, the slighter and more impressionistic handling, and the brilliant exploitation of contemporary fashion in hairdressing and other accessories reveal the native Italic taste for sharply-defined
44 character. The head of Vespasian himself (1890) is a typically straightforward rendering of the man: prosaic and efficient, with plenty of personality but not much imagination. That of his
45 son Titus is more dandified and self-conscious; the psychological effect of the neat row of curls and the chubby complacent expression is cleverly combined with the aesthetic value of rich, rounded surfaces and decoratively contrasted texture, This fine head, whose monumental scale is judiciously suited to its over-lifesize dimensions, shows how well a talented artist could make Italic character and Hellenistic form reinforce each other.

The resemblance between certain male portraits of the Flavian period and those of the late Republic is sometimes so close that many heads once thought to date from the age of Julius Caesar are now placed more than a century later. The physical type to which they tend to conform is certainly very similar, but a close examination of the technical handling is generally enough to show whether a given portrait is Flavian or Republican. The heads of the late first century after Christ are treated with a kind of fluency and ease which it would be difficult to parallel among even the most accomplished and the most Hellenistic heads of the late Republic. The form is less tight and exact in the Flavian portraits; the rendering of texture, in particular, is more atmospheric, and the artist seems to calculate his effects as though intending his work to be seen from a certain distance, not at point-blank range.

It is usual to speak of Flavian impressionism; but, as we have seen, impressionism was invented in the Hellenistic period, and

44 Vespasian.

45 Titus.

was only reintroduced into Roman art in the Flavian period when the Augustan vogue for classical precision had worn itself out. Moreover, the term 'Flavian illusionism' which found great favour some while since needs a certain amount of qualification if its real meaning is to be rightly understood. It would be more accurate to say that the realism of Flavian art is psychological rather than aesthetic in origin. The leading principle is now bourgeois matter-of-factness instead of aristocratic elegance and refinement. But the training of the Augustan period could not be altogether forgotten; and whereas the realism of Republican portraiture was objective and indiscriminate, Flavian realism was subjective and deliberate. The Flavian artist had learnt how to present his sitter not merely as an isolated individual but also as a personality with a social context. The comedy of manners appears for the first time in Flavian portraiture. Tricks of gesture and modish details are introduced for the sake of their

46 value as documents of social history; the sideways turn of the
47 head, now so popular (see 1872, 1961, 1975), implies a conscious-
48 ness of other relations beside the direct one between artist and model, and the introduction of elaborate hairdressing in the busts of fashionable women calls attention to their social rank and pretensions.

The pictorial quality of Flavian portraits is conspicuous even in their uncoloured state, and when this was enhanced with full polychrome effects, as it must once have been, the lifelike impression must have been striking. The raised and roughened surface of the hair, darkened with brown or black pigment, would produce an almost perfect illusion when seen from the correct distance; and the waxy smoothness of the marble, when treated with a wash of translucent colour, would offer an equally convincing reproduction of flesh. At the same time, however, the sculptor comes to depend less on the addition of colour and begins to experiment with the possibility of suggesting contrasts of tone and colour by purely plastic means. For example, the eyebrows, which used to be added in paint, are now raised in relief; and the eyeballs, formerly distinguished in the same way, now begin to be incised. These improvements in marble techni-que were borrowed from bronze and terracotta and gem-

46 Unknown Roman.

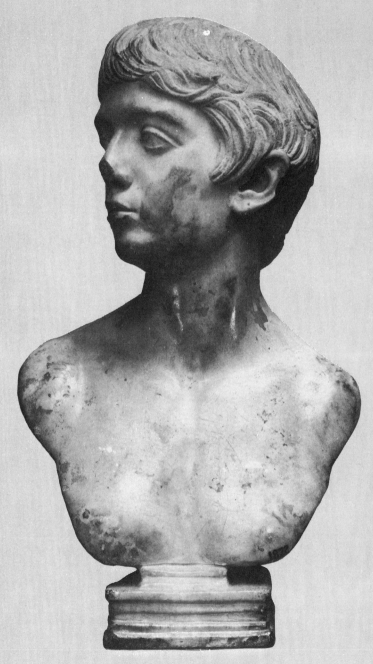

47 Unknown Roman boy.

48 Miniature bust of unknown Roman.

49 Miniature bust of Aelius Verus.

engraving, where they had long been known. This is doubtless the innovation to which Pliny referred when he said that the paintings of images had gone entirely out of fashion in his day (*Nat. Hist.* xxxv.2), though the remark, like so many of Pliny's statements about the arts, appears to be somewhat exaggerated. Not only do many Flavian portraits seem to demand the addition of colour, but unmistakable traces of pigment do occur.

The head of a man (1961) and the contemporary portrait of a boy (1872) retain their original bases. These low plinths, which appear in bronze as early as the late Republican period, seem to have been introduced into marble sculpture during the first century of the Empire. The peculiar form of the base supporting the bust of the boy, with its marble strut immediately under the head, is evidently derived from the technique of the wax *imago*; and as the unusually high polish of the surface also suggests the quality of wax, it is probable that this bust is a direct copy in marble of an original in the more perishable medium.

It is worth noting here that the size of the bust grows steadily during the first two centuries of Roman portrait-sculpture. Under the Republic and in the Augustan period it included only a small piece at the base of the neck. By the middle of the first century A.D. this had increased to a V-shaped piece of considerable size, as we see from No. 1926. In the Flavian period it spread sideways almost to the shoulders and downwards almost to the nipples; and during the second century we shall observe the bust grow until it becomes a half-length figure.

50   The honeycomb coiffure worn by the woman (1892) was popular at the court of Domitian (A.D. 81–96), where it was worn by his wife Julia, the daughter of Titus. In the next generation this elaborate artificial toupet was still further complicated by 51   rows of curls coiled like springs (see the woman from Carthage: 2006), and finally extended into a sort of turban, as in the bust of 52   Claudia Olympias (1925), a lady who is believed to have died about A.D. 115. In this portrait we observe that the bust now includes the shoulders and breasts. These tasteless fashions in hairdressing were perpetuated even in allegorical representations like that of the Apotheosis of Marciana carved in chal- 41   cedony on a miniature scale (Gems 3949), where the sister of the

64

50 Unknown Roman woman.

51 Unknown Roman woman.

52 Claudia Olympias.

53 Roman portrait-statue: Nerva?

54 Trajan.

emperor Trajan still wears her hair done in the height of fashion when borne to heaven on the back of the imperial eagle.

The sculpture of the Trajanic period continues, on the whole, the Flavian tradition, though a certain dryness again becomes noticeable, at any rate in official portraiture. The statue of an imperial priest from Cyrene, wearing the Greek himation and not the Roman toga, may possibly represent the emperor Nerva *53* (A.D. 96–8); the meagreness of the forms harks back to the early Republican period, to which, at first sight, the statue might be thought to belong. The bust of Trajan (1893) is a good represen- *54* tative example of Roman portrait-sculpture in the first half of the second century after Christ; the surface is intact and it retains its original base, and we can study conveniently the characteristic technical features of the period. The chest now includes both nipples and the whole of the shoulders. The pedestal consists of a profiled drum united to the bust by a small moulded member. This separation of the bust from its base, so unstructural in marble, shows the dependence of the sculptor on the conventions of the bronze-worker in its clearest form. Owing to the fact that so much antique bronze has been melted down, we are inclined to forget that it was once as common as marble as a material for sculpture, and always more fashionable; the most favoured artists seem to have been primarily metal-workers, and the traditions of that craft exercised a permanent influence on the carver's style. It is clear that marble was not highly regarded for its own sake under the Roman Empire; it was plentiful and tractable, and was therefore much used, but we observe that its surface was masked with paint or else polished to imitate ivory, and that its structure was ignored owing to the prevailing prejudice in favour of bronze-forms. We thus perceive that the popular notion of antique sculpture as preeminently an art of carved white marble is based upon two misconceptions; these arose at the time of the Renaissance because the great majority of ancient fragments then unearthed were of marble (the bronze having been destroyed in the early Middle Ages) and had lost their original colour through long burial. In attempting to reconstruct the antique taste from the surviving remains this contingency must always be borne in mind.

The portraits of Hadrian and his circle show the emperor's preference for the classical conventions of Attic art. These are
55 exemplified, for instance, in the statue from Cyrene (1381), where the emperor wears Greek dress and a pine-wreath, as a sign of victory in the Isthmian games. The likenesses of private persons show no such prejudice in favour of classicism, and the illusion of Flavian art develops naturally into the baroque style of the Antonine Age. The bust of Antoninus Pius from the
56 Augusteum at Cyrene (1463) shows the technical features of Antonine style fully developed—so much so, indeed, that the bust may well be posthumous. The marble is polished in the flesh parts to a vitreous finish resembling porcelain, and in marked contrast to the rough surface of the hair, which is chiselled and drilled with some elaboration, though not with any intention of appealing to the sense of touch, nor yet in the abstract decorative style of half a century later. The present rusty colour of the hair may indicate that it was once painted, or more probably gilt, in order to produce, with the ivory-porcelain quality of the flesh, an effect of chryselephantine sculpture. It is also conceivable that this finish was meant to suggest the tone and texture of a sardonyx cameo on a large scale; the influence of glyptic art has already been made partly responsible for the incision of the eyes in the marble sculpture of the second century after Christ. The
57 same features are seen in another bust from Cyrene (1910), where the colouristic treatment of the flesh and hair is combined with a metallic handling of the design for the pedestal.

The women's portraits of the mid-second century show a momentary return to simplicity after the curiosities of the
58 Flavian Age. The bust of a woman (1904), whose hair is done in the manner favoured by the elder Faustina, the wife of Antoninus Pius, shows the more normal style of about A.D. 140. Half the arm is now included, and the drapery is arranged in such a way as to avoid the awkward truncated look of the ordinary bust; simple and satisfactory as the arrangement is, it does not seem to have been universally adopted even now, although we do find it again a generation later in the bust of a
59 young man (1940) which may well represent the youthful Commodus.

56 Antoninus Pius.

55 Hadrian.

57 Unknown Roman.

The portraits of men at this period all show a profusion of curly hair, the aesthetic effect of which is achieved at first mainly by direct carving, but later by an increasing use of the drill. From being employed as an adjunct of the chisel, to lighten work and to attack deeply recessed parts which would otherwise have been inaccessible, the drill came to be used for its own sake, in order to produce brilliant decorative symbols which made no attempt to copy the growth or texture of real hair.

The finest Antonine portraits show a technical brilliance and a psychological insight which were never surpassed in antiquity. The artist of 1949, for example, an Athenian of the circle of 60 Herodes Atticus, understood with certainty everything that could be expressed by the raising of an eyebrow, the curl of a lip, or the faintest possible inclination of a head upon a neck; and he also possessed the art to plan them out and extract them from a block of marble. The vitality of this head, which abounds in intellectual as well as physical life, is Hellenic; it would be difficult to find an Italic head that showed the same reflection of the inner movements of the mind. Yet the life here is intenser and more sharply individualized than it would have been in a pre-Roman Hellenistic portrait; it is possible that this determination to extract every particle of physiognomic significance was a Roman contribution to the art of portraiture.

By comparison with its extraordinarily complete interpretation of a real person, most contemporary Italic work looks rather humdrum. The explanation of this is partly to be found in the fact that whereas 1949 is probably a portrait of an Athenian intellectual, as seen by one of the foremost artists of the day, most of the imperial portraits, such as those of Marcus Aurelius 61 (1464), Lucius Verus (1911), or Commodus (1913), were mass- 62 produced by hack craftsmen and seldom have any claim to be 63 treated as works of art. For the same reason, the best portraits of a historical personage are often those which represent him as a young man, before he became famous, and the demand for a good likeness exceeded the supply. It may be noted here that one of the finer late Antonine busts in this collection, the so-called Pertinax (1915), is probably not a portrait of that 65 short-lived emperor, but of some unknown or unidentified

73

58 Unknown Roman woman.

59 Commodus as a young man?

60 Unknown Greek.

61 Marcus Aurelius.

62 Lucius Verus.

63 Commodus.

64 Unknown Roman woman.

65 Roman General.

66 Unknown Roman woman.

67 Septimius Severus.

68 Caracalla.

general of the period. The unreliability of imperial portraits at this date is shown by the difference between two likenesses of Septimius Severus (1916 and 1944); 1916 is the canonical type 67 with the four corkscrew curls over the forehead, though it bears little resemblance to 1944, which must also represent that emperor, being over lifesize and forming a pendant to the statue of Marcus Aurelius (1906). The bruiser type of Caracalla (1917) 68 seems also to be purely conventional.

The simpler style of hairdressing introduced by the empress Sabina lasted for about half a century, with slight modifications, but shortly before 200 complex coiffures and elaborate toupets again became fashionable. A number of portraits of this period have been found with the hair made of a separate and detachable piece of marble, which could be altered with a change of fashion. This reintroduction of the wig is probably due to Julia Domna, the Syrian wife of Septimius Severus; certainly she wore a coiffure of this type, as can be seen from her coins, and it would be one of the many oriental contributions she made to Roman social life. The earliest of these new turban-like head-dresses date from about A.D. 195; a good example may be seen on the bust of an unidentified woman (1914), who was probably one of 66 the ladies of Julia Domna's court. At first we find, as here, a compact mass of hair, waved and braided, covering the ears and swathing the crown of the head. This developed in the next stage into a kind of helmet with lappets which completely covered the cheeks and enshrined the face. These, in their turn, gave place to a more becoming arrangement of ringlets, as worn by the Levantine beauty (2009) who was probably another lady of the 69 Severan court, perhaps in the reign of Caracalla (A.D. 211–18). Subsequently the ringlets were abandoned, leaving only the roll on the nape of the neck and the braiding up the back of the head 70 (1922).

It will be observed that in 2009 the bust has become a half-length figure, cut off abruptly at the waist. The arms are broken just below the elbows, and it is impossible now to guess what they were originally doing; but it is clear that they must once have been an important part of the composition, since the forearms and hands were completely detached from the body.

69 Unknown Roman woman.

70 Julia Mamaea.

This introduction of gesture as an auxiliary to facial expression was an experiment which was seldom repeated; presumably it was felt that the arms distracted attention from the face, which is by definition the reason for the bust's existence. Having reached its maximum development, the bust tended to dwindle all through the third century, reverting to the more manageable form of the Antonine period. There is one innovation which must, however, be recorded, because although not artistic in origin it had a certain influence on design. This is the trabeate arrangement of the toga, whereby a large flat fold crossed the front of the body from the right breast to below the left shoulder. This fashion, which was introduced in the second quarter of the third century, produces a strong lateral movement in the composition as an offset to the strong turn of the head to the right, which had been more or less stereotyped since the Flavian period. This balance of forces leads to a more rigid and static effect than the rhythmic pattern of folds invented by the Antonine artists in order to secure a harmonious composition. The close-cropped hair and the renunciation of picturesque accessories and technical virtuosity are other symptoms of this new and drastic style which the military emperors of the third century brought into fashion. The Antonine baroque convention was revived for a few years under Gallienus (A.D. 253–68); but in the last three decades of the century the foundations of the late-antique style were rapidly laid. Under the Tetrarchy (A.D. 284–305) the new territorial divisions of the Empire, with their capitals at Nicomedia, Sirmium, Milan, and Trier, favour the establishment of new local schools and new provincial styles; and the material can henceforth be divided up according to the East Roman, the West Roman, and the Greek spheres of influence.

The changing psychology of the Roman world and the new economic circumstances of the time can be plainly seen reflected in contemporary portraiture. The musical ease of Hellenistic art gives place to a still and abstract system of design which avoids all suggestion of physical life. The spiritual life, on the other hand, is emphasized as never before in the art of the Roman Empire. The soul is now the artist's main preoccupation, and in order to

71 Unknown Roman.

72 Unknown Roman.

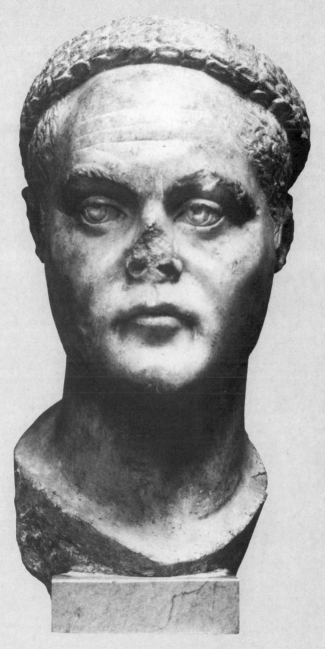

73 Unknown Roman.

74 Unknown Roman.

obtain the greatest possible expressiveness he is prepared to sacrifice a good deal of external verisimilitude. Official portraits in the old conventions still continued to be made; the man wearing the wreath (1968) may be as late as the fourth century, 73 for this head comes from Cos, where the Hellenic tradition naturally had greater powers of survival than it had in the West. But on the whole the new aim is evident. The sense of human strain, which is so characteristic of the portraits of the mid-third 72 century (1921 and 1953), is transposed into a kind of ecstasy. 71 Instead of glancing nervously over the shoulder, the eyes begin to gaze fervently ahead and upwards, out of the world. A new spirituality has descended upon man, and a conviction of the individual's insignificance. He is no longer a person, but a human unit: a soul aspiring to leave its bodily encumbrance. And so the eyes become the chief feature in the face. In the latest portraits that can still be called Roman, such as the anonymous head of about A.D. 450 (1959), they are all-important; and the other features—hair and beard, nose and forehead—have 74 become mere decorative adjuncts which frame and emphasize the only real seat of life. But we are now far from Hellenic beauty and Italic expressiveness alike; the true parallel for this remarkable document must be sought among the saints and prophets of a Romanesque cathedral.